Christmas Gifts That Won't Break
Leader Guide

Christmas Gifts That Won't Break

Christmas Gifts That Won't Break: Expanded Edition with Devotions
978-1-5018-3998-6 Book • 978-1-5018-3999-3 ePub
978-1-5018-4000-5 Large Print

Christmas Gifts That Won't Break: Leader Guide
978-1-5018-4001-2 Book • 978-1-5018-4002-9 ePub

Christmas Gifts That Won't Break: DVD
978-1-5018-4003-6

Christmas Gifts That Won't Break: Youth Study Book
978-1-5018-4004-3 Book • 978-1-5018-4005-0 ePub

Christmas Gifts That Won't Break: Children's Leader Book
978-1-5018-4006-7

Also by James W. Moore

Yes Lord, I Have Sinned, But I Have Several Excellent Excuses
Lord, Give Me Patience, and Give It to Me Right Now!
How God Takes Our Little and Makes It Much
If God Is Your Co-pilot, Swap Seats!
Have You Ever Seen a Hearse Pulling a Trailer?
Some Things Are Too Good Not to Be True
If God Has a Refrigerator, Your Picture Is on It
You Can Get Bitter or Better!
Standing on the Promises or Sitting on the Premises?
Healing Where It Hurts
Moments That Take Your Breath Away
God Was Here and I Was Out to Lunch
Are You Fired Up or Burned Out?
The Power of a Story
Finding Bethlehem in the Midst of Bedlam

Also by Jacob Armstrong

The Connected Life   Treasure
Renovate   Loving Large
Sent   Upside Down
The New Adapters   The God Story

James W. Moore
with Jacob Armstrong

CHRISTMAS GIFTS
That Won't Break

Expanded Edition with Devotions

Leader Guide
by Clara Welch

Abingdon Press
Nashville

CHRISTMAS GIFTS THAT WON'T BREAK
Expanded Edition with Devotions
Leader Guide

This book is printed on elemental chlorine-free paper.
ISBN 978-1-5018-40012

17 18 19 20 21 22 23 24 25 26 — 10 9 8 7 6 5 4 3 2 1
MANUFACTURED IN THE UNITED STATES OF AMERICA

CONTENTS

TO THE LEADER

Welcome! Thank you for accepting the invitation to lead this five-week study for adults through Advent and Christmas. You and your group of fellow learners will observe these holy seasons together as you consider *Christmas Gifts That Won't Break*. In this book, James W. Moore makes the point that God's gifts are unbreakable and eternal. In the first four chapters, he focuses on God's gifts that are represented by the four candles in the Advent wreath: hope, love, joy, and peace. In the fifth chapter, he writes about God's gift of Jesus Christ, symbolized by the white candle in the center of the Advent wreath.

This five-session study uses the following components:

- The study book *Christmas Gifts That Won't Break: Expanded Edition with Devotions* by James W. Moore with Jacob Armstrong
- This Leader Guide
- The *Christmas Gifts That Won't Break* DVD featuring Jacob Armstrong introducing and expanding upon key points from each chapter of the book.

It will be helpful if participants obtain a copy of the book in advance and read the introduction and chapter 1 before the first session. Each participant will also need a Bible.

A Children's Leader Guide and a Youth Study Book based on *Christmas Gifts That Won't Break* are available for those who wish to organize an all-church study around this program. In the back of this Leader Guide, you will find suggestions for leading an all-church study.

Consider your schedule carefully so that you will be able to hold all five sessions. You may need to begin the week before the first Sunday of Advent in order to hold the first four sessions before Christmas Day. Ideally, the fifth session will be held during the Christmas season (December 25–January 6) but a later date in January will work if you need to avoid vacation schedules.

USING THIS GUIDE WITH YOUR GROUP

As you begin your preparations, pray for the presence of the Holy Spirit to be with you and the participants in your group. No two groups are alike. This Leader Guide is designed to give you as study leader both choices and flexibility. You will find a variety of activities and discussion questions. Keep in mind the needs and interests of your group as you choose the ones you want to use. Also keep in mind the time frame you have available.

The format for each session is as follows:

Overview
- Main Topic of the Session
- Learning Objectives
- Key Scripture Passages

Prepare
- A list of things to do in advance of the session

Welcome

Opening Prayer

Open the Session
- Activity and Discussion to introduce the topic

View the Video

Engage
- Enter a deeper study of the Bible, the book, and the video

Close the Session
- Closing Activity
- Focus for the Week
- Closing Prayer

During the "Welcome" at the beginning of each session you will want to share any necessary "housekeeping" items and announcements with your group. These may include the following:

- providing information about your meeting space and parking
- outlining the course schedule
- making a comment about being faithful to starting and ending at the scheduled times
- encouraging participants to read the appropriate chapter in the book before each session
- respecting a policy of confidentiality within the group

THE ADVENT WREATH

You may want to make an Advent Wreath for use during the study. The Advent Wreath dates back to the time of Martin Luther. It is traditionally made of evergreen. The circle of the wreath symbolizes eternity. The candles may be either purple or blue. Sometimes the third candle, symbolizing joy, is pink. A white candle to represent Christ is in the center of the wreath. If you do choose to use an Advent Wreath during your study, light the appropriate candle at the beginning of each session, either before or after the opening prayer.

HELPFUL HINTS

- Before each session, read the chapter in the book and watch the video segment so that you are familiar with the material.
- Read "Prepare" in this Leader Guide several days before the session so you will have time to make any advance preparations.
- Select the activities and discussion questions that will meet the needs and interests of your group. Be open to making adjustments during the session as group members interact and other questions arise.
- Secure a TV and DVD player in advance, and be sure they are in working order.
- Prepare the space where the session will be held— choose a place where group members can see one another and discuss topics easily, either seated around a table or in a circle. Movable chairs are ideal, because the group may form pairs or small teams for discussion.

- Bring Bibles for those who forget to bring their own. It is helpful to have a variety of translations.
- For each session you will need a chalkboard and chalk, a markerboard and markers, or an easel with paper and markers for recording responses to various discussion questions.

SHAPING THE LEARNING ENVIRONMENT

- Strive to foster a sense of openness, encouraging group members to participate as they feel comfortable. Remember that some people will jump right in with answers and comments, while others need time to process what is being discussed and may take a bit longer to answer or initiate conversation. Be sure everyone has a chance to talk, but keep the conversation moving so that you stay on schedule. As the leader, it's your responsibility to moderate the meeting sessions to include everyone and prevent a few individuals from doing all the talking.
- If no one answers at first during discussions, do not be afraid of a silence. Count silently (and slowly) to ten; then say something such as, "Would anyone like to go first?" If no one responds, provide an answer yourself and then ask for comments. Or try to rephrase the question in a way that people will be able to respond to more easily.
- Model openness as you share with the group. Group members will follow your example. If you push yourself to share beyond the surface level, others will feel permission to do the same.

- Encourage multiple answers or responses before moving on.
- To help continue a discussion and give it greater depth, ask, "Why?" or "Why do you believe that?" or "Can you say more about that?"
- Affirm others' responses with comments such as "Great" or "Thanks" or "Good insight."
- Be aware of your own contributions to the conversations each session. If you find yourself doing most of the talking, back off so that you do not train the group to listen rather than speak up.
- Remember that you are not expected to have all the answers. Your job is to keep the discussion going and encourage participation.

MANAGING THE SESSION

- Begin and end on time. If a session is running longer than expected, check with the group before continuing beyond the agreed-upon ending time. Let people know that they can feel free to leave if need be.
- Note that some sessions may call for breaking into smaller teams or pairs. This gives everyone a chance to speak and participate fully. Mix up the groups; encourage everyone not to pair up with the same person for every activity.
- The study will be most successful if group members treat one another with respect and are willing to listen to opinions that differ from their own. Work to ensure that the study offers a safe space for exploring the Bible and study topics.
- Ask the group to covenant together to observe a policy of confidentiality.

Session 1

THE GIFT OF HOPE

OVERVIEW

Main Topics

Introduction—What are the Christmas gifts that won't break?

Chapter 1—How does the name of Jesus bring us hope?

Learning Objectives

Participants will:

- recognize that material gifts and objects will disappoint us,
- consider the meaning behind the names that identify Jesus, and
- discover ways that the name of Jesus brings us hope.

Key Scripture Passages

"Stop collecting treasures for your own benefit on earth, where moth and rust eat them and where thieves break in and steal them. Instead, collect treasures for yourselves in heaven, where moth and rust don't eat them and where thieves don't break in and steal them. Where your treasure is, there your heart will be also."

(Matthew 6:19-21)

This is how the birth of Jesus Christ took place. When Mary his mother was engaged to Joseph, before they were married, she became pregnant by the Holy Spirit. Joseph her husband was a righteous man. Because he didn't want to humiliate her, he decided to call off their engagement quietly. As he was thinking about this, an angel from the Lord appeared to him in a dream and said, "Joseph son of David, don't be afraid to take Mary as your wife, because the child she carries was conceived by the Holy Spirit. She will give birth to a son, and you will call him Jesus, because he will save his people from their sins."

(Matthew 1:18-21)

PREPARE

- Write the focus question for the study, "What are the Christmas gifts that won't break?" on a large sheet of paper or posterboard and display it in the room. Since this will be displayed in the room for each session, you may want to use embellished lettering or decorate the sign to resemble a Christmas gift with ribbons, bows, or shapes cut from wrapping paper.

- Set up a table near the entrance to the room with name tags and markers. Also set out Bibles and copies of the book *Christmas Gifts That Won't Break* for participants who may not bring their own.
- Write the heading "Names for Jesus" on a markerboard, chalkboard, or large sheet of paper. This will be used for an activity during the lesson.
- Have a markerboard and markers, a chalkboard and chalk, or large sheets of paper and markers available to record group responses to the various questions.
- Read the instructions for the "Hymns and Songs" activity described in the section of the lesson plan titled "Engage." Collect enough copies of your congregation's hymnal or worship music book for each participant to have one for this activity. You may also want to recruit an accompanist or song leader (see Option 1) or arrange to play recordings of selected hymns and songs about Jesus' name (see Option 2).

WELCOME

- Greet participants as they arrive and invite them to make a name tag.
- Welcome participants to this study of *Christmas Gifts That Won't Break*.
- Introduce yourself and share your enthusiasm for teaching this course. Then, briefly, in two or three sentences, tell about one of your favorite Christmas gifts you have received. It may be a gift from childhood or a more recent gift.

- Invite participants to introduce themselves and briefly (in two or three sentences) tell about a favorite Christmas gift they received.
- Share any "housekeeping" items that may be necessary for your group. See suggestions in "To the Leader" at the beginning of this Leader Guide.
- Invite participants to covenant together to observe a policy of confidentiality within the group.

OPENING PRAYER

Loving God of Hope, we thank you for this Advent season and the coming season of Christmas. We thank you for the gift of the Christ Child who brings hope to the world and to us. Be present with us throughout this study as we explore the subject of Christmas Gifts That Won't Break. *Open our hearts to receive these gifts. Show us how to share these gifts with others. We pray in the name of your Son Jesus, your gift of hope. Amen.*

OPEN THE SESSION

Call attention to the section of chapter 1 titled "Names are Important" (*Christmas Gifts That Won't Break*, pages 15–17). Share information about your name using the questions below as a guide. Then invite participants to respond to these questions:

- How did you receive your name?
- Why were you given this name?
- What does your name mean?
- How do you feel about your name?
- Does your name influence the way you think or feel about yourself? Why or why not?
- Why are names important?

VIEW THE VIDEO

Play the video for Session 1 of *Christmas Gifts That Won't Break*, titled "The Gift of Hope." After the video, invite discussion using one or more of the following questions:

- What hope do you gain from the idea that Jesus has broken down the wall that separates us from God? What does it mean that the temple veil has been torn, that nothing now holds us back from God?
- In the video, Jacob mentions that his friends Chad and Tanna are both amazing and normal, and that Mary and Joseph were both amazing and normal. How can someone be both amazing and normal at the same time? What was normal about Mary and Joseph? What was amazing about them?
- Do you think of yourself as more amazing, or more normal? Why?
- How are we included in the Christmas story? How are you and I part of the gift of hope?
- Where do you need hope? Where do you find hope this Advent?

Remind the group that as you continue your study and exploration of the Gift of Hope, everyone should keep in mind both the video and the book *Christmas Gifts That Won't Break*.

ENGAGE

Names for Jesus

Ask: What feelings do you think Joseph experienced as he encountered the angel and his message?

Call attention to the markerboard, chalkboard, or large sheet of paper with the heading "Names for Jesus." Write the name "Savior" under the heading. Explain that the name "Jesus" means "Savior."

Ask: What are other names we call Jesus? (Add each response to the list.)

Ask: What is the meaning or significance of these various names?

Add the names below to the list if they are not mentioned by participants.

- Emmanuel—"God with us" (Matthew 1:23 and Isaiah 7:14)
- Christ—anointed one (Greek)
- Messiah – anointed one (Hebrew and Aramaic)
- Wonderful Counselor (Isaiah 9:6)
- Mighty God (Isaiah 9:6)
- Eternal Father (Isaiah 9:6)
- Prince of Peace (Isaiah 9:6)
- Lord
- Redeemer
- Hope of the World

Ask: Which of these names are most meaningful to you? Why?

Hymns and Songs

Note that in chapter 1 of *Christmas Gifts That Won't Break*, James Moore mentions the gospel hymn "There's Something About That Name" by Gloria and William J. Gaither. (This is hymn 171 in *The United Methodist Hymnal*.) Distribute copies of the hymnals or worship music books you collected for this activity. (See "Prepare" at the beginning of this lesson plan.) Invite participants to use these as a resource as they respond to these questions.

> **Ask:** What other hymns or praise songs mention the name of Jesus? (List these on a markerboard, chalkboard, or large sheet of paper.)

> **Ask:** What do these hymns and songs say about the name of Jesus?

> **Ask:** Why do you think there are so many songs and hymns about Jesus' name?

Optional additions to this activity:

1. Recruit an accompanist or song leader so the group may sing several of the hymns and songs together.
2. Find recordings of hymns and songs about Jesus' name and arrange to play these for the group.

Here is a list of hymns and songs you may want to consider for this activity. Those with numbers beside them indicate the page number for *The United Methodist Hymnal*.

- "At the Name of Jesus," 168
- "O How I Love Jesus," 170
- "O For a Thousand Tongues to Sing (verse 3)," 57
- "Emmanuel, Emmanuel," 204
- "No Other Name"—Hillsong Worship

The First Advent Candle

Remind participants that the first candle we light on the Advent wreath represents hope. Call attention to the section titled "The Naming of the Christ Child" in chapter 1.

Ask: What dividing walls did Jesus break down in his day?

Ask: What dividing walls need to be broken and torn down today?

Ask: How are we able to join Jesus Christ in the work of breaking down walls that divide us from one another and from God?

Ask: How does Jesus bring hope to our world?

Ask: How does Jesus bring hope to our local community?

Ask: How does Jesus bring hope to you personally?

CLOSE THE SESSION

Closing Activity

Read, or invite a volunteer to read, Matthew 6:19-21. Then share this quote from the introduction to the book (*Christmas Gifts That Won't Break*, page 9):

> "Any one of us whose life and happiness depends on material things will surely be disappointed, because material things do not last. They go out of style. They wear out. They break."

Remind participants of the statement made by Bishop Shamblin's young son: "Daddy, my Christmas is broken already!"

Ask: What *Christmas Gifts That Won't Break* are you hoping to receive this Christmas?

Ask: What "non-breakable" gifts would you like to give to others this Christmas?

Focus for the Week

Read the "Focus for the Week" at the end of chapter 1 in *Christmas Gifts That Won't Break*, page 23.

Ask: How can you be an instrument of hope to others this week?

Ask: What opportunities do you already see to be a messenger of good news and hope to others?

Prayer

God of hope, as we journey through this holy season of Advent, may we open our hearts to receive your amazing gift of hope—hope that will not break, hope that will not disappoint us. Open our eyes that we may see others who need to receive your gift of hope and be with us as we share the hope of Jesus Christ with others. Amen.

Session 2

THE GIFT OF LOVE

OVERVIEW

Main Topic

What is Christmas and when does it come?

Learning Objectives

Participants will:

- consider how love is at the heart of Christmas;
- reflect on how we experience Christmas when we love God, love our families, and love other people; and
- explore ways we can put love into action.

Key Scripture Passage

When the angels returned to heaven, the shepherds said to each other, "Let's go right now to Bethlehem and see what's happened. Let's confirm what the Lord has revealed to us." They went quickly and found Mary and Joseph, and the baby lying in the manger. When they saw this, they reported what they had been told about this child. Everyone who heard it was amazed at what the shepherds told them. Mary committed these things to memory and considered them carefully. The shepherds returned home, glorifying and praising God for all they had heard and seen. Everything happened just as they had been told.

(Luke 2:15-20)

PREPARE

- Display the large piece of paper or posterboard with the focus question for the study, "What are the Christmas gifts that won't break?" in a prominent place in the room.
- Set up a table near the entrance to the room with name tags and markers, extra copies of *Christmas Gifts That Won't Break*, and Bibles if these will be needed.
- Write the heading, "_____ of God" on a markerboard, chalkboard, or large sheet of paper. Under the heading write in a vertical list these words: *man, woman, person, child, disciple*. This will be used for an activity described under "There Is Christmas When..."
- Have a markerboard and markers, a chalkboard and chalk, or large sheets of paper and markers available to record group responses to the various questions.
- If your congregation's hymnal or worship music book contains the song "Love Came Down at Christmas,"

collect enough copies for each participant to have one for the "Hymns and Songs" activity. If not, be prepared to read the words of this hymn to your group. You may want to recruit an accompanist or song leader.

WELCOME

- Greet participants as they arrive.
- If there are newcomers, offer a short time for introductions.
- Share any necessary "housekeeping" items. See suggestions in the introduction to this Leader Guide.
- Remind participants to observe a policy of confidentiality within the group.

OPENING PRAYER

God of Hope, God of Love, we thank you for your gift of the Christ Child. We thank you for your love made known to us in the birth of our Savior. Open our hearts to receive your love. Open our eyes to ways we may share your love with others. Thank you for each one in this group. Bless our time together as we journey through Advent to Christmas. In the name of the holy child born at Christmas we pray. Amen.

OPEN THE SESSION

Invite participants to think about a time when they experienced the gift of love and to respond to these questions with that gift in mind.

Ask: How did receiving this gift make you feel?

Ask: How did you respond?

VIEW THE VIDEO

Play the video for session 2 of *Christmas Gifts That Won't Break*, titled "The Gift of Love." After the video, invite discussion using one or more of the following questions:

- In the video, Jacob spoke about the Apostle Paul and Mother Teresa. How are the ministries of Paul and Mother Teresa connected? How do you see love at the heart of both?
- Why do you think Mother Teresa chose to talk about love in her Nobel Peace Prize acceptance speech? What does this say about her view of love?
- Do you agree that love begins at home? Why or why not? How can a more loving world begin with you?
- How is God calling you to share the gift of love this Christmas? How can it start with those closest to you?

Remind the group that as you continue your study and exploration of the Gift of Love, everyone should keep in mind both the video and the book *Christmas Gifts That Won't Break*.

ENGAGE

When We Love God, There Is Christmas

Note Moore's three section titles that proclaim that Christmas happens "When We Love God," "When We Love Our Families," and "When We Love Other People."

Read this quote from the book to the group: "The essence of Christmas is love, God's incredible love for us, expressed when he sent his only Son into the world to save us" (*Christmas Gifts That Won't Break*, page 39).

Invite a fellow group member to read John 3:16: "God so loved the world that he gave his only Son, so that everyone who believes in him won't perish but will have eternal life."

Ask: When did you first accept the truth of God's love for you?

Ask: How do you continue to grow in your understanding and acceptance of God's love?

Ask: What connections do you see between John 3:16 and the Christmas season?

Recall the story James Moore told about "the man of God" under the title "When We Love God, There Is Christmas" (*Christmas Gifts That Won't Break*, pages 39–41). You may want to invite a volunteer to summarize this story for the group. Then note that Moore suggests several words that describe our relationship with God (man of God, woman of God, person of God, child of God, disciple of God). Call attention to these words written on the board or paper with the heading "_____ of God."

Ask: What other words describe our relationship with God? (Add these to the list. Ideas are: son, daughter, servant, follower.)

Ask: Based on this list of relationships, what characterizes the life of a person of God?

Ask: How is reciprocal love (God's love for us, our love for God) at the heart of these relationships?

Ask: What are some ways we can show our love for God at Christmas? At other times throughout the year?

When We Love Our Families, There Is Christmas

Offer a brief summary of this section from the book (*Christmas Gifts That Won't Break*, pages 41–42).

[*Note to the Session Leader: Keep in mind that participants in your group may have difficult relationships within their families, and feelings about these difficulties can escalate during the holiday seasons. This course is not the proper setting for counseling, and you want to avoid the session becoming a time for "venting." As part of the discussion you may offer a general invitation to the group for individuals who have concerns about family relationships to speak with you or a minister privately.]

Lead the group in conversation about Discussion Question #3 from chapter 2 (*Christmas Gifts That Won't Break*, page 45). This is a two-part activity.

Invite participants to list some of the many ways that love of family can be shown. As members respond, write the list on a markerboard, chalkboard, or large sheet of paper. (Responses may include listening, forgiving, understanding, showing patience, being sensitive to the needs and concerns of others, offering to help with specific tasks, and praying for one another.)

Ask: What are some examples from your own experience? How have you shown or experienced the love of family? (Be mindful of the time available for this question. You may want to invite participants to share in pairs or small groups.)

When We Love Other People, There Is Christmas

Recall the story of the village cobbler (*Christmas Gifts That Won't Break*, pages 42–44). You may want to invite a volunteer to read or summarize the story for the group.

Read aloud this summary paragraph at the end of the story:

> The message of this story is a big part of Christmas: "Truly I tell you, just as you did it to one of the least of these who are members of my family, you did it to me." When we see Christ in other people and love them, then at that precise moment Christmas comes once again.

Invite participants to share stories of giving love to others or receiving love from others. Again, be mindful of your time available for this activity. If your group is large, suggest that participants share in pairs or small teams so that everyone who wants to share will have the opportunity.

CLOSE THE SESSION

Closing Activity

In the opening section of this chapter, James Moore refers to the hymn "Love Came Down at Christmas." The words were written by poet Christina G. Rossetti in 1855 (*The United Methodist Hymnal*, 242). Lead the group in recalling the words of this hymn using one of two options:

1. Distribute hymnals or worship song books to participants and invite the group to sing or say the words to "Love Came Down at Christmas" together.
2. Read the words of this hymn aloud to your group, or invite a volunteer to read the words aloud.

Ask: What does this hymn tell us about God's love?

Ask: Why is love the perfect gift?

Ask: Why is the gift of love a cherished gift?

Ask: What is Christmas and when does it come? (Moore asks this question at the beginning of this chapter.)

Focus for the Week

Direct the group's attention to the "Focus for the Week" at the end of chapter 2 in *Christmas Gifts That Won't Break* (page 47). Invite a volunteer to read this weekly focus aloud. Encourage participants to follow Moore's suggestions during the coming week.

Prayer

God of Love, we thank you for your love made known to us through the gift of the baby Jesus. Let our lives reflect the love we have for you. Let our gifts of love to our family and to other people bring glory and honor to your holy name. In the name of your Son born in a lowly stable in Bethlehem, we offer this prayer. Amen.

Session 3

THE GIFT OF JOY

OVERVIEW

Main Topic

God's gift of Emmanuel, God with us, brings us joy.

Learning Objectives

Participants will:

- embrace the joy of Emmanuel, God with us,
- recognize the ways that God is with us, and
- explore how we may share the joy of God's presence through encouragement, thoughtfulness, and graciousness.

Key Scripture Passage

> Now all of this took place so that what the Lord had spoken through the prophet would be fulfilled:
>
> > Look! A virgin will become pregnant and give birth to a son,
> >   And they will call him, *Emmanuel*.
>
> (Emmanuel *means "God with us."*)
>
> When Joseph woke up, he did just as an angel from God commanded and took Mary as his wife. But he didn't have sexual relations with her until she gave birth to a son. Joseph called him Jesus.
>
> (Matthew 1:22-25)

PREPARE

- Display the large piece of paper or posterboard with the focus question for the study, "What are the Christmas gifts that won't break?" in a prominent place in the room.
- Set up a table near the entrance to the room with name tags and markers, extra copies of *Christmas Gifts That Won't Break*, and Bibles if these are still necessary.
- On a whiteboard, chalkboard, or large sheet of paper, write the heading "Experiences of Joy." This will be used in the first activity under "Open the Session."
- Have pencils, notebook paper, posterboard or poster-size paper, and markers available for the activity described in the section titled "The Joy of Encouragement, Thoughtfulness, and Graciousness."

- If you plan to create small teams for the discussion under the section titled "Emmanuel," make copies of the questions to distribute to each team or write the questions on a markerboard, chalkboard, or large sheet of paper.
- Have a markerboard and markers, a chalkboard and chalk, or large sheets of paper and markers available to record group responses to the various questions.
- Collect enough hymnals that contain "Joy to the World" for each participant to have one for the closing activity. You may also want to recruit an accompanist or song leader.

WELCOME

- Greet participants as they arrive.
- If there are newcomers, offer a short time for introductions.
- Share any necessary "housekeeping" items. See suggestions in the introduction to this Leader Guide.
- Remind participants to observe a policy of confidentiality within the group.

OPENING PRAYER

God of Hope, God of Love, God of Joy, we thank you for your gift of the Christ Child. We thank you for the joy of knowing that you are with us. You came as a baby to live among us to give us hope, to show us your love, and to bring us joy. Open our hearts to welcome your presence and receive the joy that comes from living in relationship with you. Thank you for each person in this group and bless our time together. In the name of the holy child born at Christmas we pray. Amen.

OPEN THE SESSION

Invite participants to think about the times in their lives when they have experienced joy. Responses may cover a wide range of experiences including the birth of a child, receiving a good medical result, finding a parking space, seeing a sunrise, and celebrating a milestone event. Explain that participants will have three minutes to call out answers, popcorn fashion. Recruit one or two people to write the answers under the heading "Experiences of Joy" on the markerboard, chalkboard, or paper. Have a clock or watch available to time the three minutes.

Ask: When have you experienced joy?

After the three minutes are over, invite participants to consider the responses.

Ask: What do these experiences have in common?

Ask: What are differences among these varied responses?

VIEW THE VIDEO

Play the video for session 3 of *Christmas Gifts That Won't Break*, titled "The Gift of Joy." After the video, invite discussion using one or more of the following questions:

- In the video, Jacob mentioned that our world is weary. Where do you see the world's weariness in the news, in your own community, or in your own life?
- How does Advent lift up the possibility of joy to a weary world? What reasons for joy do we find during this season?

- The baby born in Bethlehem is a sign of God's presence, a sign that God is coming into the world to save us. How does the baby in Bethlehem move you to joy? What signs in our world right now point you toward the baby in the manger?
- Where do you need to be surprised by joy? Are you looking for a sign?
- How does giving away the gift of joy enable us to keep it?

Remind the group that as you continue your study and exploration of the gift of joy, everyone should keep in mind both the video and the book *Christmas Gifts That Won't Break*.

ENGAGE

Emmanuel

The Scripture text for this session continues the account of Jesus' birth as recorded in the Gospel of Matthew. As a review, read Matthew 1:18-21, which was the Scripture text for chapter 1. Then invite a volunteer to read Matthew 1:22-25, the Scripture text for this lesson. Invite a second volunteer to read Isaiah 7:14, which is the source of the quote in Matthew 1:23. Note these key points:

- The text tells us what Joseph did, but does not convey how Joseph felt.
- It is likely that Joseph knew Isaiah's prophecy concerning the birth of Emmanuel.

Ask: How do you think Joseph felt when he learned that God's promise of Emmanuel was being fulfilled?

Ask: How do you think Joseph felt when he realized God had called him to have a significant role in the story?

If you have a large group, you may want to create small teams for discussion of the questions below. Let participants know how much time is available for the small-group discussion. Invite the teams to discuss the following questions:

Ask: When were you first aware that God was with you?

Ask: How is God's presence made known to you in your daily life?

Ask: When is it hard to remember that God is with you?

Ask: What helps you remain mindful of God's presence?

Ask: How is the fulfillment of God's promise of Emmanuel, "God with us," a source of joy for you?

Call the teams back together. If time allows, invite each team to share briefly one or two key insights from the discussion.

The Joy of Encouragement, Thoughtfulness, and Graciousness

Note James Moore's point that the birth of Emmanuel and the truth that God is with us brings us joy. We share this joy with others through encouragement, thoughtfulness, and graciousness.

Remind participants of the three stories in *Christmas Gifts That Won't Break* that illustrate these three expressions of joy (pages 63–67). If time permits, you may want to invite volunteers to read these stories aloud to the group. These stories are found under the headings "The Joy of Encouragement" (paragraph 2), "The Joy of Thoughtfulness" (paragraphs 2, 3, 4), and "The Joy of Graciousness."

Divide your group into three teams. Assign each small team a "mission field" as follows.

- Team One: your local church
- Team Two: your city or town
- Team Three: your country and around the world

Explain that the teams will do a two-part activity. Provide each team with a pencil and notebook paper for the first part of the activity. Indicate where posterboard or large sheets of paper and markers are located if a team would like to use them for the second part of the activity. Let participants know the time frame available for working in teams and the time available for each team to present their work to the class. Offer these instructions.

1. Brainstorm responses to the following question with your specific mission field in mind and write the responses on the notebook paper provided.

   Ask: What are ways you can share the joy of "Emmanuel— God with us" in your mission field using the gifts of encouragement, thoughtfulness, and graciousness?

2. Decide on a creative way to share your ideas with the class. Suggestions are:
   - Present a short roleplay or drama.
   - Write a short story or poem for a volunteer to read.
   - Make a recruitment poster.
   - Make an advertisement poster.

○ Write and present a radio announcement.
○ Use another idea from the team.

As the teams are working, visit each one to offer support if needed and to keep each team on task. When the allotted time is over, call the whole group back together and invite each team to share.

CLOSE THE SESSION

Closing Activity

A favorite hymn, "Joy to the World" by Isaac Watts, expresses the joy of Emmanuel, God with us. Distribute hymnals that contain this song (*The United Methodist Hymnal*, 246). Note that the hymn is based on Psalm 98:4-9 and invite a volunteer to read this Scripture passage aloud. Note also that there are no specific references to Jesus' birth in Bethlehem or mention of other characters in the Christmas story as there are in other Christmas hymns.

Invite the group to sing or say the words together.

Ask: What does this hymn tell us about God?

Ask: What phrases in this hymn remind us that God is with us?

Focus for the Week

Read the "Focus for the Week" at the end of chapter 3 in *Christmas Gifts That Won't Break* (page 70). Encourage participants to follow Moore's suggestions during the coming week.

Prayer

God of Hope, God of Love, God of Joy, thank you for joy! Thank you for giving us reasons to sing and shout and leap for joy even in the midst of the most challenging circumstances. Open our eyes to the ways we may share your joy with others. In the name of your Son, born in a lowly stable in Bethlehem, we offer this prayer. Amen.

Session 4

THE GIFT OF PEACE

Overview

Main Topic

Christmas offers us peace with God, peace with ourselves, and peace with others.

Learning Objectives

Participants will:

- discern the meaning of God's peace,
- consider ways to receive God's peace, and
- commit to sharing God's peace with others.

Key Scripture Passage

Nearby shepherds were living in the fields, guarding their sheep at night. The Lord's angel stood before them, the Lord's glory shone around them, and they were terrified.

The angel said, "Don't be afraid! Look! I bring good news to you—wonderful, joyous news for all people. Your savior is born today in David's city. He is Christ the Lord. This is a sign for you: you will find a newborn baby wrapped snugly and lying in a manger." Suddenly a great assembly of the heavenly forces was with the angel praising God. They said, "Glory to God in heaven, and on earth peace among those whom he favors."

(Luke 2:8-14)

PREPARE

- Display the large piece of paper or posterboard with the focus question for the study, "What are the Christmas gifts that won't break?" in a prominent place in the room.
- Set up a table near the entrance to the room with name tags and markers, extra copies of *Christmas Gifts That Won't Break*, and Bibles if these are still necessary.
- For the activity under "What Scripture Says About Peace," write the Scripture references on individual strips of paper or list them on a markerboard, chalkboard, or large sheet of paper. Also, mark a markerboard, chalkboard, or large sheet of paper to

make three columns. Write these headings in the columns: Peace with God, Peace with Ourselves, Peace with Others.

- Have a markerboard and markers, a chalkboard and chalk, or large sheets of paper and markers available to record group responses to the various questions.
- Prepare to share the song "Let There Be Peace on Earth" with the group. You may (1) bring in a recording of this song; (2) secure a copy of the words to read to the group; or (3) recruit a soloist to sing the song for the group. If you recruit a soloist, let him or her know where you meet and when to arrive. Make arrangements for an accompanist if needed.

WELCOME

- Greet participants as they arrive.
- If there are newcomers, offer a short time for introductions.
- Share any necessary "housekeeping" items. See suggestions in the introduction to this Leader Guide.
- Remind participants to observe a policy of confidentiality within the group.

OPENING PRAYER

God of Hope, God of Love, God of Joy, God of Peace, we thank you for your gift of the Christ Child. As we journey through this holy season of Advent we are aware of our longing for peace. We long for peace in our world and in our communities where hatred, prejudice, and selfishness spark violence and suffering. We long for peace in our relationships with others when misunderstandings and hurtful actions separate us from our friends and the ones we love. We long for peace in our relationship with you when we feel separated from you by our sin and lack of faith. Open our hearts to your forgiveness and salvation. Increase our faith as we accept the gift of the Christ Child and the peace he brings. In the name of the holy child born at Christmas we pray. Amen.

OPEN THE SESSION

Invite participants to respond to the questions below, noting that there are no right or wrong answers. Write responses on a markerboard, chalkboard, or large sheet of paper.

Ask: What colors do you associate with peace? Why?

Ask: What images in nature remind you of peace? Why?

Ask: What are characteristics of a "peaceful" person?

VIEW THE VIDEO

Play the video for session 4 of *Christmas Gifts That Won't Break*, titled "The Gift of Peace." After the video, invite discussion using one or more of the following questions:

- How do we play a part in bringing the good news of peace to the world? In what ways is it our turn to do the singing, as Jacob mentioned in the video? Name one way in which you can "sing" of peace?
- In the video, Jacob contrasts peace with fear. The reassurance of "do not be afraid" is an invitation to be at peace. How are you afraid this Advent season? What do you fear?
- How does the peace that Jesus promises ease your fears?

- How does the invitation to be a part of the Christmas story bring about fear within us? How can we be at peace even though we play a part in something so big and grand?
- Where is God calling you to give the gift of peace?

Remind the group that as you continue your study and exploration of the gift of peace, everyone should keep in mind both the video and the book *Christmas Gifts That Won't Break*.

ENGAGE

What the Bible Says About Peace

Read the Key Scripture Passage for this lesson, Luke 2: 8-14.

The following Scripture verses are about peace. Ask for volunteers to read. If you wrote the individual Scripture references on strips of paper, distribute these to the volunteers. If you wrote the references on a board or large sheet of paper, assign a reference to each reader. (See "Prepare.")

- Numbers 6:24-26
- Psalm 29:11
- Psalm 34:14
- Proverbs 12:20
- Proverbs 16:7
- Isaiah 9:6
- Mark 9:50
- Luke 1:78-79
- John 14:27
- Romans 2:10-11

- 2 Corinthians 13:11
- Philippians 4:4-7

After each individual Scripture text is read, ask the following questions:

- What does this Scripture passage tell us about peace with God?
- What does this Scripture passage teach us about peace with ourselves?
- What does this Scripture passage say about peace with others?

Write responses to the questions in the three columns with the headings "Peace with God," "Peace with Ourselves," and "Peace with Others."

After all the verses are read, you may want to invite participants to share other Bible verses about peace that are helpful or meaningful to them.

Receiving Peace

Invite participants to consider and respond to the questions below. If you have a large group, you may want to create smaller teams for this discussion so everyone who wants to has the opportunity to share.

Ask: When have you needed the gift of peace in your life?

Ask: Did you receive the gift of peace? If yes, in what ways? If not, why do you think this was so?

Ask: What are some of the ways we can seek inner peace with God? (Examples include prayer, Bible study, confession, sharing with Christian friends.)

Ask: How would you like to receive the gift of peace this
Christmas?

If you created small teams for this discussion, call the
groups back together. If time permits, invite each team to
share two or three insights from their discussion.

Giving Peace

Note that peace is one of the *Christmas Gifts That Won't
Break.*

Ask: In what ways are you a peacemaker
- ❍ within your family?
- ❍ among your friends?
- ❍ with your work associates?
- ❍ within your faith community?
- ❍ in other settings?

Ask: What are factors that prevent us from being at peace
with others?

Ask: What does it mean to give the gift of peace?

Ask: What is a specific way you may give the gift of Christ's
peace this Christmas?

Let Peace Begin with Me

Share the song "Let There Be Peace on Earth" with the
group (*The United Methodist Hymnal,* 431). You may:

- play a recording of the song,
- read the words to the group, or
- invite a soloist to sing the song for the group. (See "Prepare" for instructions.)

Ask: What phrases or ideas in this song are meaningful for you?

Ask: Keeping in mind the conversation we have had during this session, what can we do to bring the peace of Christ to the world?

CLOSE THE SESSION

Closing Activity

Remind participants that James Moore has offered a "Focus for the Week" at the end of each chapter in *Christmas Gifts That Won't Break*.

Read the "Focus for the Week" at the end of chapter 1 (page 23).

Ask: How are you giving the gift of hope this Christmas?

Read the "Focus for the Week" at the end of chapter 2 (page 47).

Ask: In what ways have you practiced acts of love and kindness toward strangers during this Advent season?

Read the "Focus for the Week" at the end of chapter 3 (page 70).

Ask: How have you experienced joy during this season of Advent?

Ask: What opportunities have you had to give the joy of Christ to others?

Focus for the Week

Read the "Focus for the Week" at the end of chapter 4 (page 94).

Ask: How has this Advent study helped you prepare for Christmas?

Ask: What *Christmas Gifts That Won't Break* have your already received this Advent season?

Ask: What unbreakable gifts do you still hope to receive?

Ask: How will you continue to give the gifts of hope, love, joy, and peace during these Advent and Christmas seasons and in the seasons that follow?

Prayer

God of hope, love, joy, and peace, thank you for giving us these gifts that won't break. Thank you for the precious gift of the Christ Child, born in a lowly manger in Bethlehem. Be with us as we continue to journey through this season of Advent and as we celebrate the season of Christmas. Open our hearts that we may truly receive your gifts of hope, love, joy, and peace. Let us always be mindful of opportunities to share these gifts with others. In the name Christ we pray. Amen.

Session 5

THE GIFT OF CHRIST

Overview

Main Topic

The gift of Christ brings the gifts of faith, hope, and love.

Learning Objectives

Participants will:

- celebrate God's gift of Jesus Christ,
- claim the unbreakable gifts we receive through Christ, and
- commit to sharing Christ and Christ's gifts with others.

Key Scripture Passage

> *"Stop collecting treasures for your own benefit on earth, where moth and rust eat them and where thieves break in and steal them. Instead, collect treasures for yourselves in heaven, where moth and rust don't eat them and where thieves don't break in and steal them. Where your treasure is, there your heart will be also."*
>
> (Matthew 6:19-21)

PREPARE

- Display the large piece of paper or posterboard with the focus question for the study, "What are the Christmas gifts that won't break?" in a prominent place in the room.
- Set up a table near the entrance to the room with name tags and markers, extra copies of *Christmas Gifts That Won't Break*, and Bibles if these will be needed.
- Have a markerboard and markers, a chalkboard and chalk, or large sheets of paper and markers available to record group responses to the various questions.

WELCOME

- Greet participants as they arrive.
- Welcome participants to this last session of the study of *Christmas Gifts That Won't Break*.
- If there are newcomers, allow time for introductions.
- Share any "housekeeping" items that may be necessary for your group. See suggestions in the introduction to this Leader Guide.

- Invite participants to covenant together to observe a policy of confidentiality within the group.

OPENING PRAYER

Loving God, thank you for journeying with us through the season of Advent and bringing us to the glorious celebration of Christmas. Thank you for the gift of Jesus Christ and the wonderful, amazing, life-giving gifts we receive through him. Open our hearts to truly receive these gifts for ourselves and to share these gifts with others. In the name of your holy Son, born long ago in Bethlehem, we pray. Amen.

OPEN THE SESSION

Invite each participant to tell about one special "breakable" gift he or she received this Christmas. After everyone who wants to has shared, discuss the following questions:

Ask: Why is this gift special?

Ask: In what ways does this gift bring hope, love, joy, or peace to your life?

Ask: How will you feel if or when this gift breaks, wears out, or goes out of style?

VIEW THE VIDEO

Play the video for session 5 of *Christmas Gifts That Won't Break*, titled "The Gift of Christ." After the video, invite discussion using one or more of the following questions:

- The video recalls the story of James Moore's visit to Bethlehem, where a man told him, "Welcome home!" How does the birth of Jesus feel like home to you?

- In what ways is the birth of Jesus the foundation of the Christian faith? What other foundations are there? How is Jesus' birth related to them and distinct from them?
- In the video, Jacob calls attention to the grim details of the aftermath of Jesus' birth, Herod's orders to kill the innocent children in Bethlehem. Why is it important that we remember this part of the Christmas story?
- Where do you see evidence of brokenness and hurt in the world around us right now?
- How does such brokenness and hurt in the world point to a deep need for Jesus?
- What do you need Jesus to bring to you this year?

Remind the group that as you continue your study and exploration of the gift of Christ, everyone should keep in mind both the video and the book *Christmas Gifts That Won't Break*.

ENGAGE

"Magi came from the east" (Matthew 2:1)

Read Matthew 2:1-12.

Ask: Why did "magi...from the east" come to see the Christ Child? ("to honor him," verse 2)

Ask: How did they honor him? (with worship and gifts, verse 11)

Read this quote from *Christmas Gifts That Won't Break* (page 110):

"So, now in the spirit of humility and in the spirit of expectancy, let us go over to Bethlehem and honor the newborn king. Let us go see and celebrate the gift of Christ."

Ask: In what "spirit" do you go to Bethlehem" (Moore suggests "humility" and "expectancy.")?

Ask: How do you honor the Christ Child during this season of Christmas?

Ask: How do you celebrate the gift of Christ during this season of Christmas?

Ask: How will you continue to honor and celebrate Christ throughout the new year?

Unbreakable Gifts

Read Matthew 6:19-21, a Key Scripture Passage for Session One and this session.

Recall the unbreakable gifts that are represented by the four Advent candles that surround the Christ candle on the Advent wreath. The first Advent candle represents the gift of hope, the second Advent candle represents the gift of love, the third Advent candle represents the gift of joy, and the fourth Advent candle represents the gift of peace.

Invite a volunteer to read 1 Corinthians 13:13: "Now faith, hope, and love remain—these three things—and the greatest of these is love."

Explain that the white candle in the center of the Advent wreath is the Christ candle. Note Moore's point that Christ brings us the gifts of faith, hope, and love.

Christ's Gift of Faith

Ask: When did you first receive the gift of faith through Jesus Christ? (Some participants may identify a specific time and place. Others may have experienced receiving this gift over time.)

Ask: How has your faith grown since that time—or how does it continue to grow?

Ask: Has your faith been renewed or strengthened during these Advent and Christmas seasons? If yes, in what ways?

Invite a volunteer to read Mark 9:14-27. Note verse 24: "I have faith; help my lack of faith!" Remind participants that we are always growing in our faith and there may be times when we feel as if our faith is shaky or wavering.

Ask: Have you ever felt like the boy's father in the story and cried out, "I have faith; help my lack of faith!"?

Ask: If yes, what were the circumstances that led to your feeling that your faith was weak, shaky, or wavering?

Ask: What helped you hold on to faith or regain your faith during and after those experiences?

Ask: In general, what helps you remain faithful and continue to grow in faith?

Read John 3:16 and call attention to James Moore's comment that "This is the faith of Christmas" (page 112).

Ask: How do the words of John 3:16 offer you the gift of faith?

Christ's Gift of Hope

Ask: When did you first receive the gift of hope?

Read John 3:16 again. Note that our ultimate hope is the fulfillment of the promise that we "won't perish but will have eternal life."

Invite a volunteer to read Romans 5:5. Paul wrote, "This hope doesn't put us to shame" or "hope does not disappoint us" (NRSV). In other words, our hope in Christ for the gift of eternal life is dependable, sure, and trustworthy.

Ask: How does John 3:16 offer you the gift of hope?

Ask: What do you hope for regarding your life here on earth?

Ask: How does your confidence in the hope of salvation and eternal life influence the way you live your life?

Ask: How does your confidence in the hope of salvation and eternal life motivate you to share Christ's gifts of hope, love, joy, peace, and faith with others?

Christ's Gift of Love

In the beginning of the section titled "The Gift of Christ Brings Us the Gift of Love," James Moore mentions the hymn "Love Came Down at Christmas." This hymn was included in the session plan for session 1. Read the words to this hymn, a poem by Christina G. Rossetti.

Ask: How have you experienced God's love that "came down at Christmas"?

Ask: Why is it meaningful to you that God expresses God's love for us through the gift of the newborn baby Jesus?

Recall the story of Cathy and the doghouse (*Christmas Gifts That Won't Break*, page 114). Note that love for her puppy took Cathy into the new doghouse because the doghouse was a frightening place for the puppy. It may have been a frightening place for Cathy, too.

Ask: Where has the love of Christ taken you? (Responses may include hospital rooms, mission trips, soup kitchens, the post office to mail cards of encouragement, senior living communities.)

Ask: Where has the love of Christ gone before you to prepare a way for you?

Ask: How has God worked through the people and situations in your life to make God's love known to you?

CLOSE THE SESSION

Closing Activity

As we conclude this study of *Christmas Gifts That Won't Break*, we are also looking toward a new year.

Ask: What new blessings and insights will you take into the new year as a result of participating in this study?

Ask: How will you remain mindful of God's gifts of hope, love, joy, peace, and faith during the new year?

Ask: How will you continue to share these unbreakable gifts with others?

Prayer

Holy God of Christmas, thank you for the Christ Child. Thank you for the gifts of hope, love, joy, peace, and faith that you make available to us through Christ. As we begin a new year, help us remain mindful of your presence. Let us remember that your gifts are available to us every day. Thank you for the time that we have shared with this group. Thank you for new friendships and for old friendships that have grown stronger through our time together. Be with us now as we go our separate ways to share Christ's hope, love, joy, peace, and faith with others. Amen.

SUGGESTIONS FOR
AN ALL-CHURCH STUDY

Christmas Gifts That Won't Break encourages people to experience God's gifts of hope, love, joy, and peace during the Advent season, culminating in a celebration of God's greatest gift, the gift of Jesus Christ. These gifts never break! Author James W. Moore reminds us that material things wear out, break, erode, go out of fashion, and can be lost or stolen. He invites us to build our happiness on things we cannot lose.

A churchwide Advent program for all ages will help people learn more about the unbreakable gifts God offers through the birth of Jesus, gifts that give us more abundant life. It will offer opportunities for learning, for intergenerational projects and activities, and for reaching out to the community with hope, love, joy, and peace. The following resources are available:

- *Christmas Gifts That Won't Break: Expanded Edition with Devotions* by James W. Moore with Jacob Armstrong
- *Christmas Gifts That Won't Break: Leader Guide* by Clara Welch
- *Christmas Gifts That Won't Break: DVD*

- *Christmas Gifts That Won't Break: A Youth Study* by Mike Poteet
- *Christmas Gifts That Won't Break: Children's Leader Guide* by Daphna Flegal

SCHEDULE

Many churches have weeknight programs that include an evening meal, an intergenerational gathering time, and classes for children, youth, and adults. The following schedule illustrates one way to organize a weeknight program.

5:30 p.m.	Meal
6:00 p.m.	Intergenerational gathering introducing Advent gifts and the lighting of an Advent candle. The time may include presentations, skits, music, and opening or closing prayers.
6:15–7:15 p.m.	Classes for children, youth, and adults

Churches may want to do the Advent study as a Sunday school program. This setting would be similar to the weeknight setting. The following schedule takes into account a shorter class time, which is the norm for Sunday-morning programs.

10 minutes	Intergenerational gathering
45 minutes	Classes for children, youth, and adults

Choose a schedule that works best for your congregation and its existing Christian education programs.

ACTIVITY SUGGESTIONS

All-Church Missions Baby Shower

Ask participants to bring new baby items to give to a homeless shelter, battered women's shelter, or food pantry.

End the mission project with a party. Suggestions for snacks and games can be found in the children's study.

Family Advent Wreaths

Directions for making simple Advent wreaths can be found in Lesson One of the children's study.

Advent Candle Lighting

You may choose to use the prayers below (also found in *Christmas Gifts That Won't Break: Expanded Edition with Devotions*) as part of lighting the Advent candle during worship.

First Sunday of Advent: The Gift of Hope

Leader: "The unbreakable gift for this first Sunday of Advent is the gift of hope."

Light the first candle.

Pray: *Dear God, thank you for the season of Advent and the gift of hope. Help us to prepare our hearts for your coming and to remember the true meaning of Christmas. Amen.*

Second Sunday of Advent: The Gift of Love

Leader: "The unbreakable gift for this second Sunday of Advent is the gift of love."

Light two candles.

Pray: *Dear God, thank you for the gift of love. May we share this gift with others and learn how to love unconditionally. Help us practice love in action with family, friends, and strangers during this Advent season. Amen.*

Third Sunday of Advent: The Gift of Joy

Leader: "The unbreakable gift for this third Sunday of Advent is the gift of joy."

Light three candles.

Pray: *Dear God, thank you for the gift of joy and for the way it brightens our days. Help us give joy to others through what we say and do. Show us how to make this Christmas a true season of joy. Amen.*

Fourth Sunday of Advent: The Gift of Peace

Leader: "The unbreakable gift for this fourth Sunday of Advent is the gift of peace."

Light four candles.

Pray: *Dear god, thank you for the gift of peace. Help us put peace into practice in our lives and show others the path to true peace. Remind us to serve as peacemakers and to share the love of God with those in need. Amen.*

Christmas

Leader: "On Christmas, we give thanks for the gift of Jesus Christ."

Light the four outer candles and the Christ candle in the center.

Pray: *Dear God, we celebrate the unbreakable Christmas gifts of hope, love, joy, and peace. And most of all, we celebrate the greatest gift, Jesus Christ, your Son who came to be with us. We know that because you are here, our very lives are renewed. Give us the wisdom and courage to put these unbreakable gifts to work in our lives throughout the coming year, knowing that you are with us always. Amen.*